MUSKEGON AREA DISTRICT LIBRARY (MADL)

D0927039

MAY 1 0 2012

J 599.638   Owen, Ruth,
OWEN   1967-
             Giraffes.

DR. BOB'S
AMAZING WORLD OF
ANIMALS
GIRAFFES

By Ruth Owen

WINDMILL
BOOKS
New York

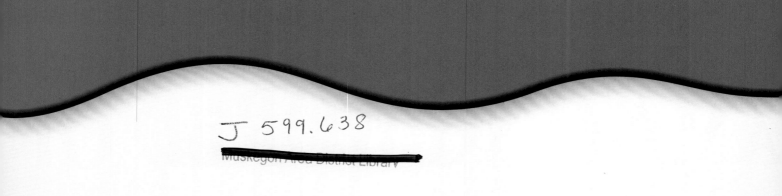

J 599.638

Muskegon Area District Library

Published in 2012 by Windmill Books, An Imprint of Rosen Publishing
29 East 21st Street, New York, NY 10010

Copyright © 2012 Ruby Tuesday Books Ltd

Adaptations to North American edition © 2012 Windmill Books, An Imprint of Rosen Publishing

All rights reserved. No part of this book may be reproduced in any form without permission in writing from the publisher, except by a reviewer.

Editor for Ruby Tuesday Books Ltd: Mark J. Sachner
U.S. Editor: Sara Antill
Designer: Trudi Webb

Photo Credits: Cover, 1, 4–5, 6–7, 8–9, 10–11 (main), 12–13, 14–15, 16–17, 18–19, 20–21, 22–23, 24–25, 26–27, 28–29, 30 © Shutterstock; 11 (top) © FLPA.

Library of Congress Cataloging-in-Publication Data

Owen, Ruth, 1967–
Giraffes / by Ruth Owen.
    p. cm. — (Dr. Bob's amazing world of animals)
Includes bibliographical references and index.
ISBN 978-1-61533-548-0 (library binding) — ISBN 978-1-61533-556-5 (pbk.) —
ISBN 978-1-61533-557-2 (6-pack)
1. Giraffe—Juvenile literature. I. Title.
QL737.U56O83 2012
599.638—dc23

                        2011027637

Manufactured in the United States of America

CPSIA Compliance Information: Batch #RTW2102WM: For Further Information contact Windmill Books, New York, New York at 1-866-478-0556

Contents

The Giraffe

Welcome to my amazing world of animals. Today, we are visiting the hot **grasslands** of Africa to meet some giraffes!

Let's investigate...

Hank's
WOOF OF WISDOM!

Giraffes are the tallest animals that live on land.

Scientists use a very old language called Latin to give animals scientific names. The giraffe's scientific name is *Giraffa camelopardalis*.

The giraffe's scientific name is made up of the words "camel" and "leopard." People long ago thought giraffes were a mixture of a camel and a spotted leopard!

The Land of the Giraffe

Giraffes live on open grasslands covered with yellow grasses. There are also some small bushes and trees.

Giraffes live in the places marked in red on the map.

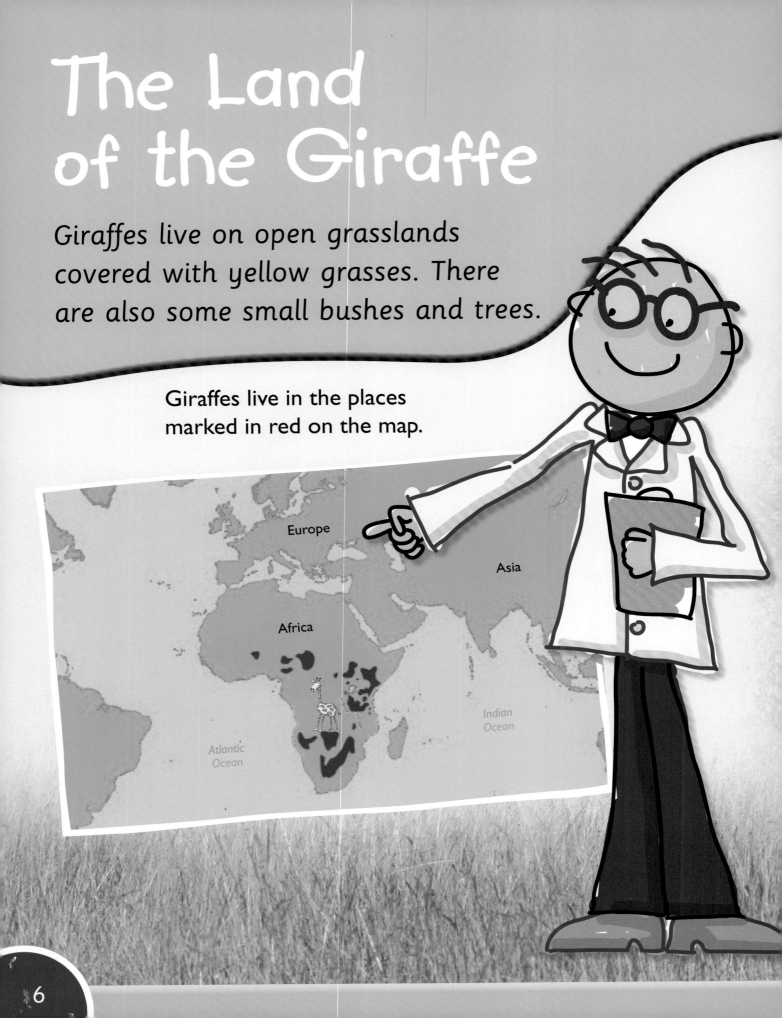

Europe

Asia

Africa

Indian Ocean

Atlantic Ocean

Adult giraffes spend time with other giraffes, but they don't live in herds.

Grassland

Around 6 to 12 giraffes may spend some time together. Then the group will split up. The group members will form new groups with other giraffes in the area.

Giraffe Bodies

An adult giraffe is tall enough to look into the second floor window of a building!

An adult giraffe's neck is about 6 feet (1.8 m) long.

A giraffe has seven bones in its neck. That's the same number of neck bones as you! The giraffe's bones are much longer, though.

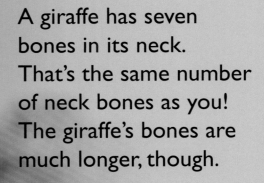

Giraffe Size Chart

Adult male giraffe

Adult female giraffe

Weight = up to 1,500 pounds (680 kg)

Height up to 14 feet (4.3 m)

Weight = up to 3,000 pounds (1,360 kg)

Height up to 19 feet (5.8 m)

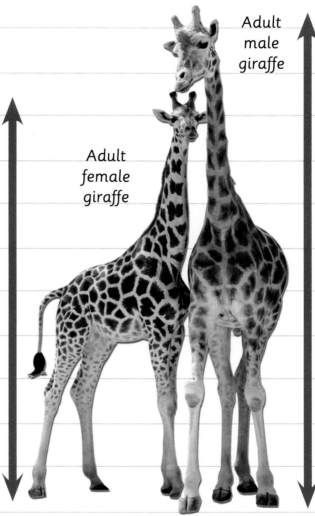

Hank's WOOF OF WISDOM!

A giraffe's legs measure about 6 feet (1.8 m) tall. That's taller than most adult humans!

Giants in Every Way!

Giraffes aren't just tall. They have many giant body parts!

A giraffe's tongue is about 20 inches (51 cm) long!

Some scientists think the giraffe's tongue is bluish black to keep it from getting sunburned when the giraffe uses it for gathering food.

Hank's
WOOF OF WISDOM!

A giraffe's heart weighs about 25 pounds (11 kg). It is 24 inches (61 cm) long!

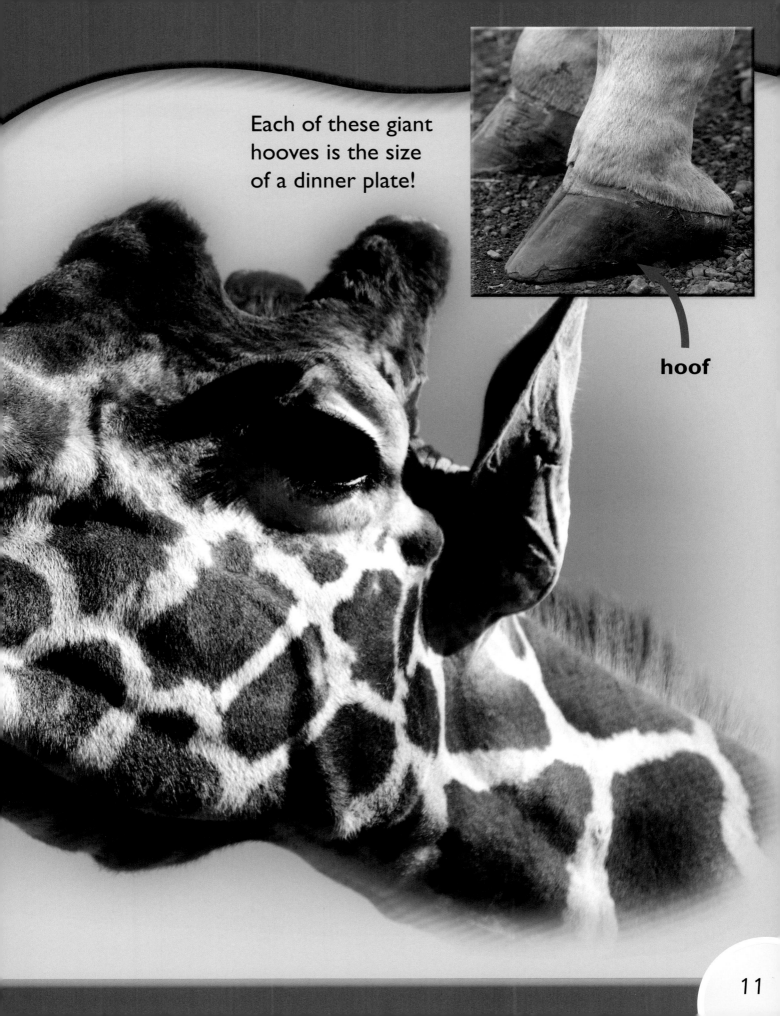

Each of these giant hooves is the size of a dinner plate!

hoof

Giraffe Jigsaws

Giraffes have a coat of short, thick hair. The coat is covered with a pattern of dark patches that fit together like a jigsaw puzzle.

Some giraffe patterns look like oak leaves

Giraffes in different parts of Africa have different types of pattern.

Some patterns look a little like a chain-link fence.

If giraffes stand close to each other, it's difficult to spot where one giraffe ends and another begins!
It's hard for a **predator** to pick a single animal to attack.

No two giraffes have exactly the same pattern.

Staying out of Danger

Unlike most grassland, plant-eating animals, giraffes have few predators. They are too large for most meat eaters to attack.

Only lions or crocodiles are strong enough to kill a giraffe.

If an adult giraffe is attacked by a lion, it can defend itself by kicking. A powerful kick from a giraffe can kill a lion!

Giraffes will also run away from predators. They have been recorded running as fast as 35 miles per hour (56 km/h).

What's on the Menu?

Leaves, twigs, and then more leaves and twigs!

An adult giraffe may eat up to 75 pounds (34 kg) of leaves and twigs in a day!

Giraffes eat leaves and twigs from acacia trees. These trees have long thorns. The thorns don't bother giraffes, though. They can twist and turn their long tongues between the thorns to grab the leaves.

Acacia tree

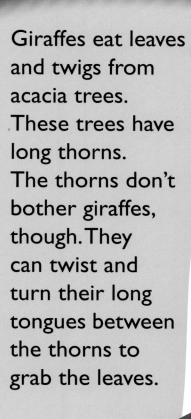

Hank's
WOOF OF WISDOM!

If a giraffe swallows a thorn, its thick, sticky spit will cover the thorn and it won't hurt the giraffe's stomach.

Chewing It Over

Giraffes have a stomach with four different compartments.

- A giraffe swallows a mouthful of chewed-up leaves. The food goes into the stomach's first compartment. Here stomach juices soften the food.

Chewing the cud.

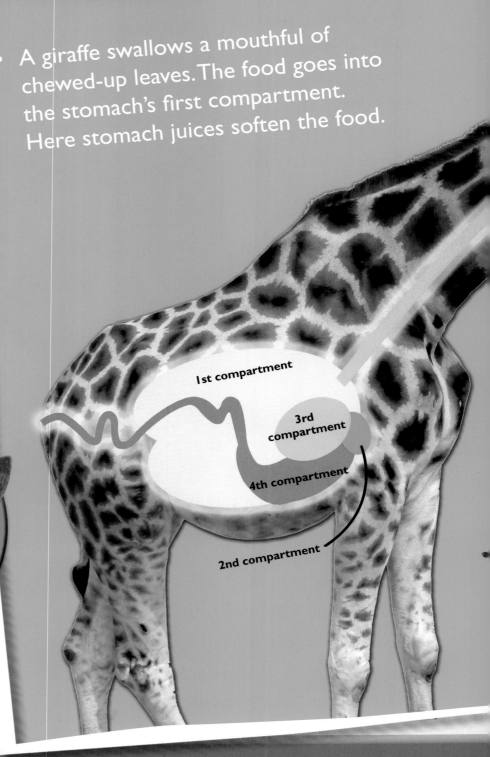

1st compartment

3rd compartment

4th compartment

2nd compartment

- The food then moves into the second compartment. It is turned into balls called cuds.

- The cuds travel back up the giraffe's throat and into its mouth. Then the giraffe chews the food all over again!

- When the giraffe swallows the cuds, they move through the other two compartments. Here, the giraffe's body takes **nutrients** from the food.

Time for a Drink

When a giraffe wants to drink some water, it has to bend down a long way!

Bending to take a drink is dangerous for a giraffe.
A lion or crocodile could attack while it is bent over.

Thankfully, giraffes only have
to drink every few days.
They get a lot of the water they
need from the leaves they eat.

Giraffes often go to **water holes** in a group.
One giraffe keeps watch for danger while
the others drink!

Lookout

Water hole

Moms and Babies

A female giraffe is pregnant for about 14 months!

A baby giraffe comes into the world with a crash!
The mother giraffe gives birth standing up. The baby drops to the ground headfirst. That's a drop of about 6 feet (1.8 m)!

The fall doesn't hurt the newborn giraffe. The shock of the fall makes the baby gasp for air and start breathing.

Hank's
WOOF OF WISDOM!

A female giraffe is called a cow. A baby giraffe is called a calf.

Predators such as lions, leopards, and hyenas attack young giraffes. The newborn giraffe must get moving fast! A baby giraffe normally stands up just 20 minutes after it is born. After an hour, it is able to walk!

A newborn giraffe is about 6 feet (1.8 m) tall.

Growing Up

A mother giraffe feeds her calf milk from her body.

Calf feeding

Calves start to eat leaves when they are around 4 months old. They still drink milk, too.

Mother giraffes will sometimes leave their calves together, like a nursery. One mother will babysit, while the others look for food.

A giraffe stays with its mother for about 15 months. Then it is ready to take care of itself. A giraffe is grown-up when it is 3 to 5 years old.

Bull Giraffes

Male giraffes are known as bulls.

Bull giraffes sometimes fight over females.
The giraffes whirl their heads around and
whack each other with their necks and heads!

This is known
as necking.

As a bull giraffe gets older, hard lumps grow on his head.

Horn

Hard lumps

Scientists think these lumps act a little like armor during fights.

Hank's
WOOF OF WISDOM!

Both males and females have small horns on their heads. Males use their horns to butt one another during play fights.

The Future for Giraffes

There are around 80,000 to 100,000 giraffes living in the wild in Africa.

Unlike many wild animals in Africa, most types of giraffes are not **endangered**. Their numbers may be dropping, though.

There are nine different types of giraffe. Scientists think one type, the Rothschild's giraffe, may be in trouble. There may be fewer than 400 of these giraffes left.

Scientists are studying giraffes and the places they live. They are also trying to count all the giraffes. This information will help us figure out what needs to be done to protect giraffes in the future.

Glossary

endangered (in-DAYN-jerd)
In danger of no longer existing.

grasslands (GRAS-landz)
A hot habitat with lots of grass and few trees or bushes. Sometimes it is very dry, and at other times there is lots of rain.

nutrients (NOO-tree-ents)
Substances that a living thing needs to help it live and grow. Foods contain nutrients such as vitamins.

predator (PREH-duh-ter)
An animal that hunts and kills other animals for food.

water holes (WAH-ter HOHLz)
Ponds or other places where there is water for animals to drink.

Dr. Bob's Fast Fact Board

Some scientists think giraffes have their jigsaw pattern to camouflage, or hide, them among trees and bushes. This makes it hard for predators to spot a giraffe.

Giraffes make mooing, hissing, roaring, and whistling noises.

A giraffe is a ruminant animal. Ruminants chew their food twice and they have four stomach compartments. Other ruminants include cows, sheep, goats, llamas, and camels.

Zookeepers have seen giraffes in zoos drink up to 10 gallons (38 L) of water in a day!

Web Sites

For Web resources related to the subject of this book, go to:

www.windmillbooks.com/weblinks

and select this book's title.

Read More

Bredeson, Carmen. *Giraffes Up Close*. Zoom in on Animals. Berkeley Heights, NJ: Enslow Elementary, 2008.

Sackett-Smith, Lucy. *Giraffes: Towering Tall*. Mighty Mammals. New York: PowerKids Press, 2010.

Shea, Mary Molly. *Giraffes*. Animals That Live in the Grasslands. New York: Gareth Stevens Publishing, 2010.

Index